S0-EGH-125

SACRAMENTO PUBLIC LIBRARY
828 "I" Street
Sacramento, CA 95814
04/15

Scavengers:
Eating Nature's Trash

Raccoons

Emma Carlson Berne

PowerKiDS press

New York

Published in 2015 by The Rosen Publishing Group, Inc.
29 East 21st Street, New York, NY 10010

Copyright © 2015 by The Rosen Publishing Group, Inc.

All rights reserved. No part of this book may be reproduced in any form without permission in writing from the publisher, except by a reviewer.

First Edition

Editor: Joanne Randolph
Book Design: Joe Carney
Photo Research: Katie Stryker

Photo Credits: Cover Danita Delimont/Gallo Images/Getty Images; p. 5 Karl Umbriaco/iStock/Thinkstock; pp.7, 8 Purestock/Thinkstock; p. 9 Chris Wolf/iStock/Thinkstock; p. 10 1bluecanoe/Flickr/Getty Images; p. 11 Aksenova Olga/Shutterstock.com; p. 12 Hans-Walter Untch/E+/Getty Images; p. 13 EBFoto/Shutterstock.com; p. 14 Tony Campbell/iStock/Thinkstock; p. 15 Zoonar RF/Thinkstock; p. 16 Fuse/Getty Images; p. 17 GlobalP/iStock/Thinkstock; p. 19 Thomas Kitchin & Victoria Hurst/First Light/Getty Images; p. 20 John_Galt111/iStock/Thinkstock; p. 21 Warren Price Photography/Shutterstock.com; p. 22 Daniel J Cox/Oxford Scientific/Getty Images.

Library of Congress Cataloging-in-Publication Data

Berne, Emma Carlson, author.
 Raccoons / by Emma Carlson Berne. — First edition.
     pages cm. — (Scavengers: eating nature's trash)
 Includes index.
 ISBN 978-1-4777-6597-5 (library binding) — ISBN 978-1-4777-6598-2 (pbk.) — ISBN 978-1-4777-6599-9 (6-pack)
 1. Raccoon—Juvenile literature. 2. Scavengers (Zoology) — Juvenile literature. I. Title.
 QL737.C26B43 2015
 599.76'32—dc23
                    2013049390

Manufactured in the United States of America

CPSIA Compliance Information: Batch #WS14PK6: For Further Information contact Rosen Publishing, New York, New York at 1-800-237-9932

Contents

All About Raccoons

Have you ever woken up to find that someone or something has knocked over your trash can in the night? You nighttime visitor likely was a furry, masked raccoon. It was trying to get at the garbage inside your trash can.

Most people know raccoons only as furry troublemakers. These mammals are clever and **adaptable**, though. They can open all sorts of lids and latches. They can live almost anywhere, even when people take over their natural **habitat**. They can eat just about anything, too, including food thrown away by people and dead animals. Raccoons are **foragers**, hunters, and **scavengers**.

Raccoons are known for the black, masklike markings on their faces. They are also known for getting into people's garbage cans!

Raccoons, Raccoons Everywhere

Most raccoons are found in North America. This is their native home. They live in all 50 states and in Mexico and Canada. The only places they don't live are the highest mountain ranges and the Arctic. Raccoons have been introduced to a few countries in Europe.

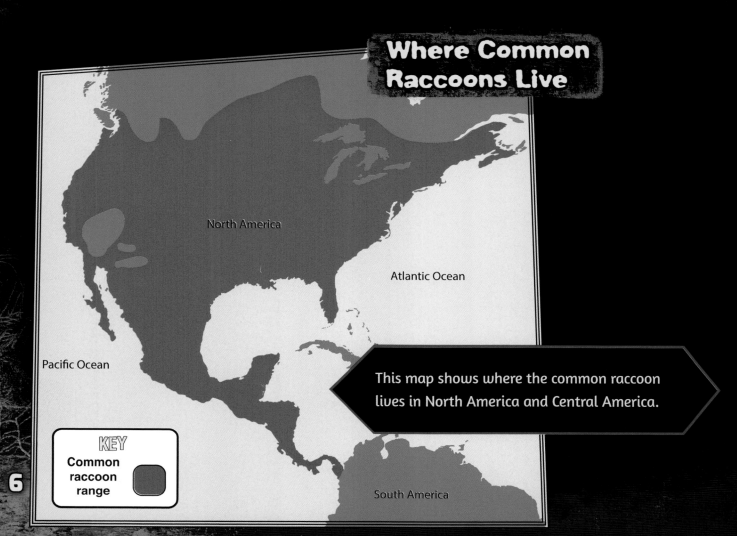

Where Common Raccoons Live

North America

Atlantic Ocean

Pacific Ocean

South America

KEY
Common raccoon range

This map shows where the common raccoon lives in North America and Central America.

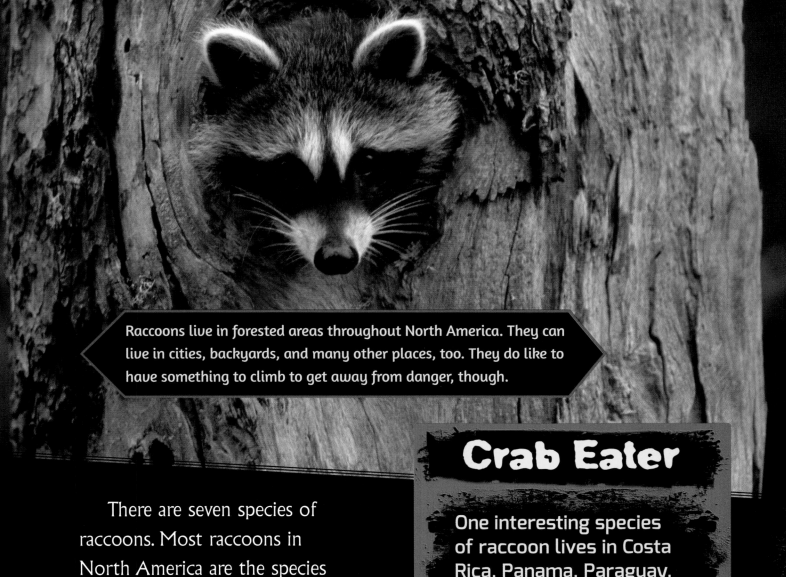

Raccoons live in forested areas throughout North America. They can live in cities, backyards, and many other places, too. They do like to have something to climb to get away from danger, though.

There are seven species of raccoons. Most raccoons in North America are the species *Procyon lotor*. Other species live on Barbados and on islands off the coast of Mexico. The crab-eating raccoon lives in parts of South America and Central America.

Crab Eater

One interesting species of raccoon lives in Costa Rica, Panama, Paraguay, Uruguay, and northern Argentina. This type of raccoon is **semiaquatic** and eats crabs, fruit, insects, and small animals. It has less fur than the common raccoon because it lives in warmer climates.

7

Adaptable Animals

If they have food, shelter, and water, raccoons can live just about anywhere. They can live in deserts, forests, farm fields, cities, and suburbs. Raccoons prefer to live near water. They drink a lot of water and like to wash their food in water, too.

Raccoons choose habitats based on whether there is water nearby. They need it for drinking and washing their food. Raccoons are excellent swimmers, too.

Raccoons are able to hunt for food, but they prefer food that is easier to come by. That is why people's garbage is so tempting.

Raccoons make little temporary homes just about anywhere. They might live in tree holes, hollow branches, city sewers, abandoned squirrel or bird nests, under porches, or inside chimneys. They use this home as a base and search for food from there. Then, in the winter, they find a more permanent den to sleep in, usually a hollow tree.

Masked and Striped

A raccoon has two special features. It has the black mask that runs across its face and its bushy ringed tail. These beautiful markings are there for a reason. Like football players' black face paint, the mask cuts down on glare, especially at night. The mask also helps raccoons see in the dark. The black fur absorbs any light that might be around, such as moonlight.

Raccoons cannot see in color, but they can see very well in the dark.

Most raccoons have between five and eight dark stripes on their tails.

Raccoons use their handy tails to prop themselves up when they stand on their hind legs. This helps them balance when they climb. They also store fat in their tails to help them get through the winter.

Water Lovers

Raccoons have very sensitive feet. Their front feet can feel as well as a human hand. Raccoons have five toes. There are three longer toes in the middle and two short ones behind. Their paws are strong enough to climb trees and **nimble** enough to undo latches.

Raccoons have very sensitive feet. They can use them to climb, open shells or trash cans, and much more.

Raccoons love to wash their food in water. Scientists think that this is because the water makes raccoons' paws more sensitive. They can feel the food better and learn more about what they are about to eat.

Fun in the Water

Raccoons will hold interesting objects underwater to examine them. Sometimes, they just dangle their paws in water, even when they aren't holding anything.

What's for Dinner? Anything!

Like many animals, raccoons are **omnivores**. They can eat just about anything. Their diet might include crayfish, clams, frogs, turtles, berries, acorns, wild fruit, insects, earthworms, snails, all kinds of fish, birds, ducklings, eggs, chickens, nuts, and all kinds of seeds. They will really eat any plant or animal that is available and edible! Of course, raccoons are happy to snack on human food scraps, pet food, or livestock feed, too.

Raccoons especially like cat food because it often has a fishy smell, and raccoons love to eat fish.

Raccoons spend a lot of their time looking around for food. They will eat nuts, berries, and fruits when they cannot find animals or insects to eat.

Raccoons eat as much as they can in order to gain weight from late spring through fall. Then, in winter and early spring, when there's not much food around, raccoons use up their fat stores.

Bandits!

Raccoons are smart, crafty, and good at opening lids and latches with their strong, nimble paws. They are easily able to live near people. Naturally, raccoons love to eat food people leave behind.

Raccoons have become quite good at opening up garbage cans. They are smart and willing to work at it until they figure it out.

Raccoons will eat eggs they find in nests, but they will eat the leftovers they find in human garbage, too.

Raccoons can be a nuisance to farmers and gardeners. They will break into sheds or barns and gorge themselves on food that is not put away. They'll raid gardens and fields of crops and pluck fruits and vegetables right from the vine. Near people's homes, raccoons are experts at getting into garbage cans and tearing open bags for the tasty discards inside.

Smart Scavengers

Raccoons love to hunt fish and insects and forage for fruit and grain, but they are scavengers, too. If other food isn't available, raccoons will eat **carrion**, garbage, or rotting plants.

Raccoons didn't always eat human garbage, though. Humans have taken over more and more of raccoons' natural habitat. There are fewer streams with fish and shellfish. There are fewer forests where they can find nuts and seeds. Rather than dying from lack of food, raccoons in suburbs and cities have switched their diets to discarded human food since it is what is available.

People regard raccoons as pests because they often make a mess as they search trash cans for garbage.

Being a Baby Raccoon

Adult raccoons **mate** in midwinter. Then the female raccoon goes back into her den. In the spring, she comes out to have her babies.

Raccoon babies are born in groups of two to seven. They are only about 4 inches (10 cm) long at birth. The mother nurses and cares for them, leaving them only to hunt for herself.

Mother raccoons generally have litters of three or four babies at one time, though they can have more or less. The young stay with their mother for several months.

The young learn how to find food and shelter from their mother. The father has no role in caring for the babies. These two raccoon kits wait for their mother to return.

After about a month, the cubs begin to climb out of the nest. They learn to run and climb trees. They play fight with their littermates. When their mother goes hunting, the babies follow her and watch what she does. This is how they learn to

We Need Raccoons

Raccoons are part of the vast life cycle on Earth. These clever mammals might knock over your garbage cans at night, but they also eat insects that harm crops. By eating fish and rodents, they keep these animals from overcrowding streams and forests. Raccoons eat dead animals that otherwise would pollute our ground and water.

Raccoons themselves are food for coyotes, wolves, and owls. Like all animals, raccoons have an important place in our huge, fragile **ecosystem**.

Raccoons help get rid of garbage that would otherwise sit around and rot.

Glossary

adaptable (uh-DAPT-uh-bul) Able to change to fit new conditions.

carrion (KAR-ee-un) Dead, rotting flesh.

ecosystem (EE-koh-sis-tem) A community of living things and the surroundings in which they live.

foragers (FOR-ij-erz) Animals that hunt or search for food.

habitat (HA-buh-tat) The surroundings where an animal or a plant naturally lives.

mate (MAYT) To come together to make babies.

nimble (NIM-bul) Quick when moving.

omnivores (OM-nih-vorz) Animals that eat both plants and animals.

scavengers (SKA-ven-jurz) Animals that eat dead things.

semiaquatic (seh-mee-uh-KWAH-tik) Lives partly in the water.

Websites

Due to the changing nature of Internet links, PowerKids Press has developed an online list of websites related to the subject of this book. This site is updated regularly. Please use this link to access the list: www.powerkidslinks.com/scav/coon/